CRANBERRY HEART

DR. ARNAB CHATTERJEE

Made with ♥ on the Notion Press Platform
www.notionpress.com

To my Muse, who visits me each day: twice

Contents

Contents

Preface

Cranberry Heart breaks my lull as a poet after a long gap of over a year and also makes me complete penning over five hundred poems. It is true that my much-acclaimed book *Guernica,* written after the Ukrainian-Russian war and which, as some of my fellow poets have adroitly pointed out, contains a strong anti-fascist statement was published this year, but I faced a writer's block for some time. Having left my native state, a doomed place of empty promises, I relocated to a new one, for the reasons that life probably had to offer me much still, as all was not over, even though the suffering in my soul goes on and will probably, for ever. When I arrived, it was a new place, with faces and just faces. I was terrified and slowly gave it a try—relocation to a new province, also called "internal diaspora", is not easy; just as to an international location is—you have to change a lot of your mental furniture. I was busy doing that. And this consumed much of my time. Months passed and slowly the faces became familiar, the iron in the soul gave way to feelings kindred and I was absorbed in the ebb and flow of the tide at workplace that consumes my six days a week. But those six days are worthwhile, they give me the purpose of existence and the reasons why I left the flowers, the "hibiscus of my echoing, bellowing land." Though I missed my people, I told myself that I had to carry on. And I carried on.

There has been an eternal literary debate whether poetry 'suffers' in service of social commentary or not. I have never thought of that very carefully, as I believe great poetry is penned both in mellower times and in “blood and darkness”. Poetry is a synthesis. A reconciliation of the heart and the intellect in the metaphysical tradition. And best words in their best order. But the best comes out when you have a Muse. The famed nine daughters of the Greek God Zeus, the Muses have inspired poets ever since. But the Muse can be anything—even your reflection in the mirror in the morning and the consolation that the image that you see therein can change your day is your Muse. She need not be a woman per se. It can be anything, a sensation that makes you write. But this time, it is a woman whom I admire and who is special. The one whose company I cherish as a friend and a man. And who cherishes mine (I hope so). And thus, one evening, after the thunderstorms had ravaged the skies, I thought of giving it a try. But my fellow poets know well that you need inspiration, that you need the “milk of paradise” to write. Good poetry is not just filling pages, it is much else. It is an intense realization, a remembrance of things past, present and future. The ruminations on questions eternally confronting mankind. Then, something happened after the rains. I scribbled a poem. I knew she is my Muse, and she does too. That is the best part. But then, you need a theme to write. What ought to be the stuff on which my dreams would be built?

And thus, I decided something queer, something that I thought should find memorable expression in my verses. I relied on my feeble powers of observation and contemplated her, as one would Nature or the rare sunset on Hawaiian Islands. I found themes and they came in galore. The friendship and the company we enjoy. The feelings of joy, sorrow and trust that we discern in each others' eyes. The intense realization that this is the best she can get, and also a fear that all will melt in the throes of the corroding influence of time. The latter sensation exhausts me and turns me delirious. But nothing can beat the present. And I told myself that the present has to be enjoyed. And so, we enjoy. The Muse is ever present, in flesh and blood, in her sensations of thirst and gloom, the excellent, tender hands that harbour the innocence of the "Byzantine times", in the soft voice that charms and captivates me and makes my eyes scan whenever she is far away. This she knows and so, for the first time, the poet and the Muse are one. There is no need to beg for inspiration, for she *is* the stuff, that subtle inspiration personified. She is all when I write—life, death, gloom, sorrow and hope. And Nature. But maybe, while I pen this rather long, rambling preface, as I am still penning these poems, I might get stuck. Just a touch of her crystalline palms on the manuscript will rekindle the spontaneity that mark these verses. This, I am sure of. And she will not refuse, for she is a little creature, longing for life and love, in a world that barters dusty death for what you hold dear. Thus, each poem is a "chapter" indeed, singing a saga of love, gloom and despondency.

Cranberry Heart marks the culmination of such thoughts. That come from the depths of the earth. Here I write directly, earthily, and have shed much of the artifice and the mawkish sentimentality of my previous verses. I celebrate our companionship, and since that is without illusions, so should these verses be. Nothing can be far from truth. These are honest epithets.

---Dr. Arnab Chatterjee

Vaddeshwaram

Vijayawada--- 522502

Andhra Pradesh State

India.

+91-9330473173

<carnab393@gmail.com>

Acknowledgements

To Nishi di and Tim for reviewing the book amid their busy schedules

Chapter1

CRANBERRY HEART

Cranberry heart
limbs of wheat,
the hairy rice and husk
overgrown in multitude—
singing lullabies with lilies
in a field of hay.
Great is the river of life
our promises, that tender hand
which I once touched,
and a Muse sprung
transparent.
Under the tree of gloom
we sit, trembling like a leaf
in the noon of coppery sunshine.
Just three and a half feet away
your realm starts
and I—
swearing the fruits of joy
the heart of gold
and a brazen life
full of upward running rivers,
watch.

Your second arrival is due—
I travel through flora
and the deep seas
holding seasons in my lap
and you arrive.
I gather my best parts,
fossilized, disintegrated.
I awake in an iridescent room
humming my last, best song.

Chapter2

WHEAT AND RICE-I

Rice and wheat
burnt flakes and dead leaves,
even a passing sensation—
vie for your smile.
Like noon bearing lust
greed and gravel;
pregnant with the lilacs of gloom,
the sea twirling endurance
emptying its foam in a blind
kitten's eyes.
Thus, battling the hours
the enigma of arrival and farewell,
the sweat, the fluid of the seasons
along with the blood red hibiscus
of my echoing, bellowing land—
rice-like
with wheatish sensations;
drunk with the thorns
and brambles of a burnt, lost civilization,
I vie for your smile.

Chapter3

WHEAT AND RICE-II

Juxtaposed, like brothers-in-arms
rice and wheat lie
in blazing sunshine, in torrid agriculture
of an alien land.
The rivers move
along the circle of faith
over the thin brows
of your mid-day life
over semi-cracked lips
spurning doomsday
through faith and faithfulness.
Like a swollen fruit—
you announce the congruity of life
and manners.
While far away,
Juliet sells flowers
within a compass of derision and laughter.
Wheat and rice mix
like we do, in strange places
afraid to roam and dip
in currents full of sharks
belching an erstwhile meal of pomfrets.

And the great vegetation sings
when you walk, on a carpet
you do not know of—
the invisible one;
thus, trampling silence.
While, nearby,
cherries sing
in bountiful harvest
when wheat and rice groan
at the failure of the sun.

Chapter4

I DO NOT START THE DAY

I do not start the day
with questions or an unchained agony—
those that tirade till death
or, list what you love or hate.
Into the deep furrows of your parted hair
within the depths of your cranberry heart,
that beats all into silence and rhapsody—
I do not address straw-like questions
of your cravings and abhorrations.
I listen to you. Just,
when you enter,
still, like the sky parched
awaiting the thunder, the applause
the kiss or the rude denial
of the firmament.
And then,
I listen to you,
like I did often—
when, in the evenings of my boyhood,
I shaked the wild, berry tree
and waited for the fruit's fall—
deep into the leaves;

full and free.

Chapter5

ENDURANCE

The arrival,
the damned arrival,
the murky, dusty, emaciated arrival—
does not happen.
Within narrow lanes
the earth revolves
and spins out of orbit.
I wait.
The dead groan
the thorn kisses the dew
a tombstone is discovered,
the savages are kissed.
Like a pressure on the equator
the cosmos forces itself on me.
I endure.
Seas rebel, the land is out of sight;
in the holes in the skies
left by dying stars
the bats swirl.
I persist.

Chapter6

LET THE DROSS PASS

Let the dross pass—
slither, evaporate.
Hide it somewhere,
in the closet, in
the salty ruminations of the room
in the sudden darkness of the noon,
within the crucifix of desire;
beside the fallen hair
of a marauding canine
under the eyelids of a failed stare.
In the hymns of the midnight,
gloom falls, evil rises.
Put it there, choke it
within those balmy palms
that harbour the nails of a child
still and intransigent.
Let the dross pass
tonight, somewhere
under the sewers of a lost city
in the memory of desire
within the lanes of a topaz civilization
screaming under the terrain at last.

Strangle it with your smiles
that quick shake of your head,
that hunger in your heart
and the desire for arrival again—
deep, from the depths of the soil.
Let the dross pass, evaporate
wiggle between those fingers
deep into the mist of a day,
in love with life and death.

Chapter7

I FEAR THE FINAL HOUR

That final hour
like stars and clouds
or blackened faces
desperate for a hide
will come.
In the midst
of an excellent chaos
that portends a parting
amid a crowd of sound and frenzy
the final hour shall arrive.
Our souls shall part
and shadows will transfix
in the midst of a ship
high on the seas,
in the blue skies
of desire and dread.
Within the tulips of a lurid youth
swinging in the wave of life,
we'll meet the last time.
I fear the final hour—
in the coppery glass of merchandize, in
the noon of lust

in the throes of separation
drinking steel in days,
of a vanquished civilization.

Chapter8

FORSAKEN

Forsaken
like a yellow hair on a white face
or a thorn on a plate of fish,
there's nothing like a lone soul
swimming in the midst of tenderness.
In the height of noon
when the doors are closed
to keep out the sun
a forsaken soul walks,
braving the hot winds
treading burning diamonds
to the tower of bliss.
Forsaken lilies burn
in the height of the day
till pearls and rubies walk
to kiss the frost.

Chapter9

A TRUCE

An agreement, a truce
is a sordid thing.
Lying scattered in tin cans, or
with discarded locks
near the sewer.
Your mere shake of the head
dusting rumination out
will lead us nowhere,
playing fire
with frightened kittens.
At the crack of dawn—
the earth rises, and
this vegetation agrees with
the torn hibiscus, bleeding
though, still smiling.
The blowing wind shall charm
the dead in forgotten rooms,
no forced truce, no duress
can extract a chilling shriek from them.
A quick shake of your head
without the wisdom of the stars
will merely lead to the mire

under the lotus or lilies.
Thus, tired
we both smile
and pronounce the end of the day—
tearing the unwritten truce
of pertinence to minutiae,
and feeding it;
to a blind mongrel
near that lane.

Chapter10

RUDE HOURS

Watered by the tears of the sun
fanned by the ignorance and innocence
of a thousand years
the tender hand revolves.
Just five inches wide
your palms smell
of an ointment, I had no idea
even existed.
But those rude hours
filled with brambles!
I encircle your arms
the white fountains
of a decimated past
and pronounce you—
But those rude moments
filled with serpents!
Through the multi-coloured glass
of life and manners
we walk,
in the twilight of a fading dusk
announcing a hearth or a head
for the dark.

And it all ends—
the glory of this rendezvous
the cool breeze, that dries my forehead
the death of my former, wicked self
the birth of as child from the trees
or,
the roots.
But those vile hours
filled with ache!

Chapter11

BROKEN COMPASS

Broken compasses hang
on dry grass—
announcing doom
in dusty clocks.
The poles shudder
at the approach of the sun
the moon weeps
at the approach of the
burning, simmering sea.
Somewhere, Coriolanus screams
And Caesar belches.
We don't mind.
* * *
A funeral hangs in the air
announcing a new birth;
reverse, the earth spins
and, in the dizzy day
the wolves weep and sleep.
We don't care.

Chapter12

WITNESS

As a torn cloth on the walls
I am a witness
of the moon hanging on the lips
reading forgotten scripts.
High, on the roof
I wander, in genteel company—
while, in an obscure room
you sit, sneezing and sleeping.
A great tide of time flows
turning rocks into dust.
I walk, and the world moves—
while upstairs, you miss this drama of life
the acid insanity, the terrible loss
of honey and wine.
These gods whisper, and I sing
a song that I hate
in glittering glasses.
I glimpse my face,
in an alien land
mummifying history
in caskets of fruits.
Like a bright flame

your smile revolves
in the room of your faith,
while I wander
on alien shores
for a dusty merchandize.
A fool among the dunces
a fabric hiding sores.

Chapter13

GULLS MOVE

The cranberry heart bleeds
at the approaching wave.
Just three feet away
You sit.
While gulls move above
announcing the dawn
deep in the grace
of your being.
But.
The rude day sets in
under a coppery sky, —
and thus begins,
the delirious barter of life.

Chapter14

RUDE MANGOES

Rude mangoes,
and broken branches;
after the hail,
the rain
and,
the aroma,
of the final destruction.
Only your arrival
will inundate the famished road,
like the fluid of the stars
awaiting the lake.

Chapter15

CANOPY

Like the canopy
of a tree, eager
to take the fruit in its embrace—
my hands move towards yours,
a soldier's hands
a worker's hands
the hands of a liar
a hand eager for the hand,—
and,
your little ones move towards mine.
A seed within the fruit.
A child in the womb.

Chapter16

FEET

Hard feet
hard, bony feet.
The feet of a child—
the legs of a forgotten past
the limbs of a groaning civilization,
awaiting a marauding foe.
They walk on earth
finding solace
through the seas of turbulent faith.
Till we meet.
And they have met me;
and that's the end
to your sojourn—
through streets
of a dreadful past.

Chapter17

I MET A CHILD

I met a child with braces on.
A small creature came,
dressed in a mundane outfit.
My eyes moved
And were silent.
The girl looked on,
the eyes moved
and my cruel stare remained diffident.
Now, the lady moves through these lines…
My fingers tremble
and eyes scan.

Chapter18

HOLD ME

Hold me
I told her—
She did.

Chapter19

AT FOUR IN THE NOON

At four in the noon
something strange happens.
Is it evening or noon?
Is it the hard slap of the day
on the soul of the faithless one?
At four in the even-noon,
an aura arrives
a moment stops
time freezes.
Scorpions die, the earth spins out of orbit.
At four at the appointed hour
something happens!

Chapter20

WOUNDED EYES

Wounded eyes
and a hungry soul
have no parallel.
Like a road of a dusty hamlet
or a hidden pass,
within the oaks or the sycamores—
wounded eyes hide secrets.
At the appointed hour
they are discovered
when the twain meet each other;
and a kindred wound is found.

Chapter21

A THOUSAND

A thousand destruction wrought
with a hammer of gloom and doom,
the vegetation groaned
and leaves withered.
In the lake
beyond the hill,
emerged a face
with pale eyebrows
and dark eyes.

Chapter22

ANEW

A journey through the lanes
interspersed with trees
and monkeys
displaying insipid tricks.
We move.
The lanes exhaust finally
and,
we're anew,
still...

Chapter23

THE CRANBERRY MATES

Seriousness and mirth play
in tandem.
The Cranberry mates with the peach.
In a field full of wildflowers—
the world moves, and multiplies...
We look on.

Chapter24

WORDS

Your words
the syllables
the tone and the pitch.,
the momentum of faith,
the crystalline innocence
of the Byzantine times.
It's a potter's clay
or, the wheel
the fullness of your being,
the edge of a lost topaz,
the smile buried in time's blaze
through a groan
and centuries of mirth.

Chapter25

HALF-AWAKENED EYES

Half-awakened eyes
look for the clock
and announce
the fact—
that you lost track of time.
While below,
Somewhere
time stops
a heart longs for a garden of calendulas.
Beneath the green moon
shadows swoon.

Chapter26

ABSENCE

Even the absence for a day
is a meteor hurtling—
eager for Armageddon.
The oceans boil
branches swirl in,
a being disappears
in strange sands.
That absence of a day
makes him paint his face in black—
an alienation sought
in familiar faces.
A friend turned foe
in celebrations.

Chapter27

LOVE

Love sought
in strange shores—
in a crowd of prying eyes,
is a succulent tomato;
pierced by a nail gone blunt—
or a cabbage decimated
by a guillotine.
Like a dark shadow
forsaking a frame—
we seek the vegetation;
in arid scapes.

Chapter28

DEEP DESPAIR

In deep despair
within a glassy regret
the windows crack—
the sky harbors scorpions.
Ships sink, faith crumbles.
the very current of life,
is a hell.
In deep despair,
within the bushfire
of a forsaken union
when she is far away—
a blackened ground is prepared;
for a hasty burial.

Chapter29

THE HEAVEN IS THE EARTH

All the heaven is the earth
all the earth is the sky
and,
all the sea is the ink;
all the land is the horizon.
Within your deep embrace
in times of pestilence—
all disease is a bliss
and grace is doom.

Chapter30

DEATH IN THE AFTERNOON

Death in the afternoon
the disintegration of the intellect,
this myopia of perspective
the utter erosion
of the senses.
The world moves
in a snail's dwelling
evil flies with the hawk's wings—
while we move
with measured steps
eager to save the crystalline dreams
from a fool's shadow.

Chapter31

DYING STAR

Gloom descends
on the clouds,
when you arrange a journey away.
In the shade of an impending freedom—
slavery stands
with shackles of smoke
rent from a dying star.

Chapter32

A FARMER

A farmer went
to sow seeds
to bring forth a child,
from the depths of earth.
In burning agriculture
amid the sneezing rains
a farmer went—
to dig for furrows.
From your head to your feet,
it's a long journey—
a curve down the plateau
a twist in the rivers.
A farmer suffered
as he lost the way
in the secret pathways
of your predicament.
In the mellow sadness of those eyes
in the deep caverns
of those ears.

Chapter33

RUDENESS

Rudeness
is what you probably do not know.
A rancour is alien to you
like a blemish on a pristine cosmos.
I wonder,
how you do this—
can a child dreaming in the wind
or a rhapsody on a breezy night
with all its might,
compare this utter alienation?
Sneers, scorns
you're oblivious of,
as the incense is
in a room—
with the worshippers
far away
in strange tides.

Chapter34

DO NOT LEAVE EVEN FOR A MOMENT

Do not leave
even for a moment.
Do not forsake
the tulip conversation
for a silly run for conveyance,
that transports you—
to a glass palace
full of hours;
that crawl backwards
and pronounce the silly beginning of time
when the old, the happy old
refuse to grow young—
for the paltry existence,
in brazen sheds.
Just, do not leave
even for a moment,
it's a sky full of serpents then,
the topaz shatters into glass
the clock is decimated,
and—
in the evening of the sunset
in the height of a violent, mellow spring

when souls sing—
it's dead, unyielding winter.

Chapter35

SEASCAPE

Like the waves on the pebbled shore
as the foam, the furious weather
the ebb and flow of the sea.
The chemistry of time
with the acuity of the Maker.
Like a single grain of salt.
sand and the shells
we're one.
And beneath the sea? —
nothing lies.
It's all dead there
like a man
inhaling smoke
on mad, March days.

Chapter36

FRIENDSHIP

This friendship
this communion of the hearts
the soul and the mind.
Where does this come form?
The stars? The deep well within?
From the remnants of a great love saga?
Or,
a desire to wrest whatever
we can—
in recalcitrant times?
The summer burns
the winter freezes
under the dying, waning moon
love rekindles itself.
Friendship is like the thin slice of bread,
on overflowing butter.
Or, a peanut tossed on a fruitcake.
Like the oaks of wilderness, it stands
while the storms blow all
till the leaves whimper.

Chapter37

COMPANIONSHIP

Companionship
like the deep marigolds
in the echoing garden.
Like a meteor tossed in the skies
as the dew caught in the hourglass.
In the twilight of the days
our companionship revolves
like we do
in dusty lanes.

Chapter38

DEATH ON ROSES

In the height of the noon
a dream revolves
like a fragment of sunshine.
When eyes are clenched
or when the fist locks.
Outside, the light dances
on the leaves,
on the impossible shores
of life.
In torrid and burning desires,
to be one.
In the heat of the day
you arrive, —
and, all is well
like death on roses.

Chapter39

WHERE?

Where the clouds?
Where the trees?
Where is—
the terrible beauty of the sunshine
playing hide and seek
in baleful littorals?
In the midst of life
we're in death.
In the canopy of the night
darkness revolves
and sin rises.

Chapter40

THE UNIVERSE

The end finally comes,
slithers, evaporates.
Like the mid-day fumes.
A parting advice is passed,
and the universe fuses.

PRAISE FOR THE BOOK

1. An everyday charm characterizes the poems in *Cranberry Heart* that speaks of the regular, the mundane in expressions that linger on. The poems also reveal a searing pain, an angst that tears out. This juxtaposition brings out the myriad colours that life is all about in a language that is simple and speaks on several levels. Life and its negotiations emanate in various expressive ways in the poems in this volume creating a chiaroscuro of emotions that remain long after one has read them.

--- Dr. Nishi Pulugurtha

Poet, Academic and the author of *The Real and the Unreal.*

2. I have read Arnab's poems and I wonder who she is! I have only three words to describe the poems—passionate, sensuous and deep. Undoubtedly, the work of a genius. Whoever, she be, she deserves to enter the line of illustrious Muses ranging from Laura, Beatrice to Maltide Urrutia.

--- Tim Esther Delaware

Canadian poet and critic.

ABOUT THE AUTHOR

Dr. Arnab Chatterjee is an Associate Professor of English at the Centre for Distance & Online Education, Koneru Lakshmaiah Education Foundation (Deemed to be University), Vaddeshwaram, Vijayawada, Andhra Pradesh; India. He has penned poems, a dystopian novel, short stories, academic books and a volume of critical essays. He is the author of *In Desolate Dwellings, Residence Beneath the Earth* and the long narrative poem *The Wind in the Abyss,* that make up *The Reflections Trilogy*. An alumnus of St. Xavier's College, as well as Presidency College, Kolkata, his name appears in the prestigious *Who's Who of Indian Writers Writing in English* (ISBN: 978-81-260-4812-0), a nation-wide record of writers compiled by The Sahitya Akademi, New Delhi, the National Academy of Letters of India. He has penned over eleven volumes of poetry, some of which have been published and others awaiting publication. His hobbies include listening to music, academic research, writing and travelling. His book *Language Across the Curriculum: A Sourcebook for Student-Teachers* (ISBN: 978-81-934600-54) has been much appreciated within the academic circles in West Bengal and beyond and the second edition is well underway. His recent books include *The Golden Harvest* and *September Songs* (poetry), a book of drama, *The Meeting & Other Plays*, the recent *A Violent Spring & Other Poems*, and lastly, his magnum opus *Footnotes of History: A Tale of the Mahabharata*. He is active on social media and maintains his own book blog "PDF" (Poetry, Drama, Fiction). His verses have appeared in *The Ijagun Poetry Journal, Muse India* and the prestigious *The Blue Nib Poetry Magazine*. His poetry, as it has often been pointed out, is marked by multi-layered imagery, freshness of voice and a "broad philosophical outlook", deftly fusing the transcendental and mundane. He sits in the editorial and the advisory board of the prestigious journal, *The Kolkata Arts*, previously known as *The Quiver Review*. *Guernica* is his latest book of poems. He can be contacted at +91-9330473173 and carnab393@gmail.com/carnab393@kluniversity.in .Read more of his books at <https://www.amazon.in/ArnabChatterjee/e/B082RCC25Y%3Fref=dbs_a_mng_rwt_scns_share>

READ MORE BY THE SAME AUTHOR

All titles available at major e-commerce stores

1. ***Footnotes of History: A Tale of the Mahabharata***

<https://www.amazon.in/Footnotes-History-Mahabharata-Arnab-Chatterjee/dp/9390266653>

2,000 BC. Early Iron Age India. Large tracts of lands lie uninhabited. Slowly, large settlements like Hastinapur appear on the horizon and a thriving place of commerce and trade is established. But with development comes its associated costs—greed, covetousness and false pride. Plots are hatched and common people groan. Dhritarashtra, peaceful, snug, like a "slimy frog" in a pond rules for some years. Shakuni, with his own untold, tragic tale, refuses to take care of his kingdom of Gandhara, somehow overseen by his two sons now, a province grown impeccably corrupt though. Caste system remains rigid and yet, Eklavya slays all the Kuru brothers in rage and revives them at the behest of Dronacharya, who is rather keen on the restoration of his pupils' lives than a mere piece of flesh. Draupadi, bored of the false pride of her five husbands confesses her secret love for Karna. During the War of Kurukshetra, Bhanumati's condition worsens, while Vikarna, the third Kaurava shows his battle skills much before the *dharma yuddha*. Sahadeva's fore-knowledge of the war and the infamous game of dice shocks many. *Footnotes of History* is an attempt at re-telling the most destructive war depicted in Hindu mythology and asks us again what it really means to be a "footnote" in the pages of dusty history, awaiting re-discovery.

2. *A Violent Spring & Other Poems*

<https://www.amazon.in/Violent-Spring-Other-Poems/dp/9390266327>

In an irate world full of confusions and its miasma, the spring finally comes. It has to. But Nature responds not in the way it should. The screams of the world and the dilapidation of the human spirit mar with the first buds that sprout. There are "muffled cries" here and there. As if an unnecessary foliage spoils the flowers of life as weeds do. Thus, the fulcrum of perfectibility is burnt to ashes.

A Violent Spring & Other Poems captures this silent malady inherent in existence, in whatever we do. Gaps continue to sprout in the way history is narrated; lovers, perfectly content with themselves ultimately find this tranquility illusory, a sub-tropical storm shows that nothing will be the same again, no matter what we do. If the limiting factor is human nature and the uncertain world wherein we eke out a routine, then springs will continue to be violent, regeneration will be short-lived and Banquo will eternally return, failing not this feast of life and death.

3. ***The Golden Harvest***

<https://www.amazon.in/Golden-Harvest-Arnab-Chatterjee/dp/9388942353>

The book is yet another addition to the many volumes of poetry that the author has penned. Working on multifarious themes ranging from nature, God, love, separation, the mechanics of existence and time, the poet ponders on the issues that confront mankind daily. Contemplative and yet not sermonizing, these poems try to capture the very essence of existence and being. The poems are fresh, sensitive and it is the reader who is ultimately called upon to judge so. They are the “Golden harvest” of the poet’s mind and soul.

4. ***The Meeting & Other Plays***

<https://www.amazon.in/Meeting-Other-Plays-Arnab-Chatterjee/dp/1674651066>

These plays do not convey much, nor do they seek to demonstrate in the traditional sense. They are not "well-made plays" in the strict sense of the term. In one, a meeting that seeks to solve the issues of day-to-day affairs of a residential society sees supernatural beings joining in, but their serio-comic inclusion deepens the complexity further. In yet another, a nondescript man suddenly becomes the center of attention, hitherto neglected, and confined to the fringes of human civilization. In the third, the Devil himself gives an altogether new, albeit mock conception of hell and heaven and becomes one with the mundane and the brazen. Whatever be the ‘vision’ of the dramatist, these plays with three different, yet recognizable backgrounds just give an image of what may happen. The dividing line between reality and illusion is blurred and nothing seems to be impossible. Using a somewhat magic-realist mode, they show the seemingly bizarre, commonplace.

5. ***Guernica***

<https://www.amazon.in/-/hi/Dr-Arnab-Chatterjee/dp/9356289336>

Guernica. That terrible loss and pain. The enigma of existence. A heap of broken images. These poems encapsulate the essential absurdity of modern life, the ruminations on issues eternally confronting humankind. Each poem is not a finished tale, but loose ends within that narrative. The poet never stops from fusing bits and starts of mental images hewn from a plethora of sources, no matter how mundane they seem. The midnight blues. The fall of the guava leaves. A bark that destroys everything. The desire to renew manifests itself in these lines that speak the inherent nobility of the human spirit and the insignificant cries amid which it is surrounded. The Guernica. That has neither a centre nor a well-defined anchor. Just whirlpools of sorrow. The Guernica.

COMPLETE READING LIST

Poetry

In Desolate Dwellings

Residence Beneath the Earth

The Wind in the Abyss

The Golden Harvest

September Songs

Penitent Night: A Book of Haiku Poetry

Footnotes of History: A Tale of the Mahabharata

A Violent Spring and Other Poems

Guernica

Plays

The Meeting & Other Plays

Academic Books

Language Across the Curriculum: A Source Book for Student-Teachers

Egalitarianism, Gender & the Educational Framework

J.M. Coetzee's Foe: A Thematic Analysis [forthcoming]

Language Teaching & Learning [forthcoming, with Dr. Debabrata Hazra]

Novels

P.: A Novel

Visit:https://www.amazon.com/Arnab-Chatterjee/e/B082RCC25Y?

Printed by Libri Plureos GmbH in Hamburg,
Germany